Oct 2018

THE BALD EAGLE

by Brittany Cesky

Cody Koala

An Imprint of Pop!
popbooksonline.com

abdopublishing.com
Published by Pop!, a division of ABDO, PO Box 398166, Minneapolis,
Minnesota 55439. Copyright © 2019 by POP, LLC. International copyrights
reserved in all countries. No part of this book may be reproduced in any
form without written permission from the publisher. Pop!™ is a trademark
and logo of POP, LLC.

Printed in the United States of America, North Mankato, Minnesota

042018
092018

THIS BOOK CONTAINS
RECYCLED MATERIALS

Cover Photo: iStockphoto
Interior Photos: iStockphoto, 1, 14; Shutterstock Images, 5 (top), 5 (bottom
left), 5 (bottom right), 6, 13, 17, 19, 20; North Wind Picture Archives, 9, 10

Editor: Meg Gaertner
Series Designer: Laura Mitchell

Library of Congress Control Number: 2017963469

Publisher's Cataloging-in-Publication Data
Names: Cesky, Brittany, author.
Title: The bald eagle / by Brittany Cesky.
Description: Minneapolis, Minnesota : Pop!, 2019. | Series: US symbols |
    Includes online resources and index.
Identifiers: ISBN 9781532160455 (lib.bdg.) | ISBN 9781532161575 (ebook) |
Subjects: LCSH: American bald eagle--Juvenile literature. | Signs and
    symbols--United States--Juvenile literature. | Emblems, National--
    Juvenile literature.
Classification: DDC 929.9--dc23

Hello! My name is
Cody Koala

Pop open this book and you'll find QR codes like this one, loaded with information, so you can learn even more!

Scan this code* and others like it while you read, or visit the website below to make this book pop.

popbooksonline.com/the-bald-eagle

*Scanning QR codes requires a web-enabled smart device with a QR code reader app and a camera.

Table of Contents

A National Symbol

The bald eagle is a **national symbol** of the United States. It is a symbol of strength and **independence**.

Watch a video here!

The bird is respected and well liked for its beauty and proud look. It only lives in North America. So it is special to the United States.

History

The United States claimed its independence in 1776. The US **Congress** wanted a national symbol for the new country. But no one had a great idea.

Complete an activity here!

Then congressman Charles Thompson suggested a bald eagle. Congress liked it. The bird became a national symbol in 1782.

Other suggestions included scenes of soldiers and shields.

Chapter 3

The Great Seal

The bald eagle is seen on the Great Seal of the United States. The bald eagle holds arrows in one foot and an olive branch in the other.

Learn more here!

The bird holds a banner in its beak. The banner says "one from many" in Latin. This means that many states make one country.

The bald eagle as a national symbol is found in many places. It is on US money. It is on government papers.

Chapter 4

Protected Bird

Laws protect the bald eagle. People cannot hunt bald eagles or take a nest or egg without a **permit**.

Learn more here!

People also cannot keep eagle feathers. These laws keep eagles safe. America's national symbol can keep flying in the sky.

Native Americans are allowed to keep eagle feathers.

Making Connections

Text-to-Self

Do you think another bird would have made a better national symbol? Or do you agree with the Founding Fathers' choice?

Text-to-Text

Have you read other books about US symbols? What do the symbols stand for?

Text-to-World

How do the laws about bald eagles affect people in the United States today? Do you think the government should keep protecting bald eagles?

Glossary

Congress – the part of the US government that makes laws.

independence – freedom from the control of other people or things.

national – having to do with a nation.

permit – a piece of paper giving someone permission to do something.

symbol – something that stands for something else because of how they are similar.

Index

Online Resources

popbooksonline.com

Thanks for reading this Cody Koala book!

Scan this code* and others like it in this book, or visit the website below to make this book pop!

popbooksonline.com/the-bald-eagle

*Scanning QR codes requires a web-enabled smart device with a QR code reader app and a camera.